JUST 4 KIDS

JUST 4 KIDS

LOVE FOOD

Love Food ® is an imprint of
Parragon Books Ltd

Parragon
Queen Street House
4 Queen Street
Bath BA1 1HE, UK

Design: Terry Jeavons & Company

ISBN 978-1-4075-3388-9

Printed in China

This book uses metric and imperial measurements. Follow the same units of measurement throughout; do not mix metric and imperial. All spoon measurements are level, unless otherwise stated: teaspoons are assumed to be 5 ml, and tablespoons are assumed to be 15 ml. Unless otherwise stated, milk is assumed to be full fat, eggs and individual vegetables such as potatoes are medium, and pepper is freshly ground black pepper.

Recipes using raw or very lightly cooked eggs should be avoided by children, the elderly, pregnant women, convalescents, and anyone suffering from an illness. Pregnant and breast-feeding women are advised to avoid eating peanuts and peanut products.

Contents

Introduction

If you find it a challenge to get your children to eat nutritious home-cooked food, then *Just 4 Kids* is the answer. With recipes specially written with children in mind, the book is an indispensable guide to making food that children will actually eat. Many of the recipes will appeal to adults too, thus eliminating the need to cook separate meals for parents and children. For parents at home with children, the book contains plenty of ideas for attractive dishes to tempt babies and toddlers, as well as more sophisticated fare for older siblings.

The book begins with breakfast, the most important meal of the day and the one that is often the most difficult to get school-age children to eat. The recipes have been chosen to tempt children in a hurry or with little appetite, but there are also substantial dishes for those who start the day feeling ravenous.

Good-quality protein in the form of meat, poultry and fish is vital for growing children and teenagers. The recipes include a fantastic selection of tasty dishes from around the world, guaranteed to satisfy all ages and appetites. The vegetable recipes ingeniously combine mildly-flavoured or sweet-tasting varieties with ingredients such as beans and pasta, so your children will hardly know they are eating them. The recipes are also perfect if you have a vegetarian in the family.

There is an all-important chapter devoted to healthy snacks, both sweet and savoury. The trick is to have snacks ready when needed, so your children will be less likely to demand sugary sweets and drinks. Sandwich fillings and dips such as hummus can be made in advance and stored in the fridge. Popcorn and nachos can be made in minutes and are fun for children to help with. The book finishes with a wonderful selection of delicious treats that your children will love, whether it's rice pudding for everyday eating or a spectacular sundae for a special occasion.

When time is short, it often seems easier to opt for ready-prepared convenience foods. However, there is no denying that food freshly prepared at home is likely to be much better for your children and the rest of the family too. By making food from scratch you know exactly what's going into it and you can plan meals so that your children get the most nutritious food for their particular stage of physical development.

It's a good idea to encourage your children to help you in the kitchen. By involving them in a few simple tasks or letting them cook a recipe from start to finish (with a little parental guidance), you will help develop a life-long interest in good wholesome food.

1 Breakfast

An energy-rich breakfast makes a nutritious start to the day, especially important for school-age children. Creamy porridge or muesli with nuts and dried fruit will keep energy levels stable until lunchtime, as will a cooked breakfast of scrambled or baked eggs. Chilled smoothies and yogurt are easy-to-eat options for those in a hurry. Fruity muffins or fruit-and-nut bread make a change from toast, and will be popular with all ages and tastes.

Fruity Purple Oatmeal

INGREDIENTS

serves 4

100 g/3½ oz fresh or thawed frozen summer fruits such as raspberries, strawberries, blackcurrants, redcurrants, cherries or blackberries

25 g/1 oz rolled oats

100 ml/3½ fl oz milk

1–2 tsp honey (optional)

natural yogurt, to serve (optional)

1 Take half the summer fruits and process to a purée using a hand blender. Put the oats and milk into a small saucepan and simmer gently for about 5 minutes, stirring from time to time. Cool a little and stir in the honey, if using.

2 Pour into a serving bowl and stir in the fruit purée, making a swirling pattern. Roughly chop the remaining fruit and scatter on top. Serve with natural yogurt, if using.

Muesli Muffins

INGREDIENTS

100 g/3½ oz ready-to-eat dried apricots, chopped

4 tbsp orange juice

2 eggs

155 ml/5 fl oz soured cream

100 ml/3½ fl oz sunflower oil

85 g/3 oz light muscovado sugar

280 g/10 oz self-raising flour

1 tsp baking powder

TOPPING

55 g/2 oz light muscovado sugar

55 g/2 oz crunchy muesli, lightly crushed

25 g/1 oz butter, melted

makes 12 large or 36 small muffins

1 Preheat the oven to 190°C/375°F/Gas Mark 5.

2 Put the apricots and orange juice into a small bowl and leave to soak for about 15 minutes. Put the eggs into a bowl and beat. Add the soured cream, oil and sugar. Add the apricot mixture and stir well. Put the flour and baking powder into a bowl and gently stir in the egg and apricot mixture but do not over-mix.

3 Spoon the mixture into paper cases in a muffin tray. Mix together the topping ingredients and sprinkle over the top of the muffins. Bake for about 10–15 minutes for small muffins and 25–30 minutes for larger muffins.

Smoothies

INGREDIENTS

serves 2

FRUIT SMOOTHIE

½ mango, peeled and chopped

1 small banana

4–6 strawberries

100 g/3½ oz Greek-style yogurt with added honey

150 ml/5 fl oz milk

4 ice cubes

MALTED BANANA SMOOTHIE

1 small banana, chopped

200 ml/7 fl oz milk

2 tbsp malted milk powder

4 ice cubes

FRUIT SMOOTHIE

1 Put all the ingredients into a blender and process until smooth. Pour out and serve with straws.

MALTED BANANA SMOOTHIE

1 Put all the ingredients into a blender and process until smooth. To make a chocolate variation use chocolate malted milk powder and chocolate ice cream. Pour out and serve with straws.

Coconut Muesli

INGREDIENTS

15 g/4 oz porridge oats

115 g/4 oz wheat flakes

3 tbsp raisins

55 g/2 oz dried unsulphured apricots, finely chopped

55 g/2 oz roasted hazelnuts, finely chopped

25 g/1 oz desiccated coconut

freshly grated apple (optional)

makes 10 portions

1 Mix together the oats, wheat flakes, raisins, apricots, hazelnuts and coconut. Store the mixture in an airtight container.

2 Just before serving, mix a few spoonfuls of the muesli with 2 tablespoons of freshly grated apple, if liked, or serve on its own.

ABC·123

Baked Eggs

INGREDIENTS

butter, for greasing

2 large eggs

2 tbsp single cream

salt and pepper

serves 2

1 Generously butter 2 small ramekins and break 1 egg into each dish. Season well with salt and pepper and spoon over 1 tablespoon single cream.

2 Place the dishes in a roasting tin with enough hot water to come halfway up the sides of the dishes and bake at 190°C/375°F/Gas Mark 5 for 15 minutes for a soft egg and 18–20 minutes for a firmer egg.

Blueberry Bran Muffins

INGREDIENTS

150 g/5½ oz plain white flour

100 g/3½ oz light brown self-raising flour

1 tbsp oat bran

2 tsp baking powder

½ tsp bicarbonate of soda

pinch of salt

50 g/1¼ oz demerara sugar

1 tbsp clear honey

1 large egg

200 ml/7 fl oz buttermilk

150 g/5½ oz fresh blueberries

makes 10

1 Preheat the oven to 180°C/350°F/Gas Mark 4. Line 10 holes of a muffin tin with muffin paper cases.

2 Mix the flours, bran, baking powder, bicarbonate of soda and salt together in a bowl and stir in the sugar. Whisk the honey, egg and buttermilk together in a jug.

3 Pour the wet ingredients into the dry ingredients and stir briefly to combine. Don't overmix – the mixture should still be a little lumpy. Fold in the blueberries.

4 Spoon the mixture into the paper cases and bake in the preheated oven for 20 minutes, until risen and lightly browned.

5 Remove the muffins from the oven and leave to cool in the tin. Serve warm or cold.

Sunshine Toast

INGREDIENTS

serves 1

1 slice granary or wholemeal bread

1 tbsp olive oil

2–3 mushrooms, sliced

1 tomato, halved

1 small egg

pepper

1 Using a biscuit cutter, cut a hole in the centre of the slice of bread, large enough to hold the egg.

2 Heat the oil in a non-stick frying pan and cook the mushrooms and tomato, cut-sides down, for 3–4 minutes, until the mushrooms are beginning to brown. Turn the tomato over.

3 Make a space in the middle of the pan and add the bread. Crack the egg open and carefully pour it into the hole in the bread. Reduce the heat and cook slowly until cooked through.

4 Season everything to taste with pepper and serve the sunshine toast with the mushrooms and tomato alongside.

Crunchy Yogurt

INGREDIENTS

serves 1

200 g/7 oz rolled oats

2 tbsp clear honey

2 tbsp pumpkin seeds

2 tbsp sunflower seeds

2 tbsp chopped walnuts

1 small ripe pear, peeled, cored and chopped

½ ripe mango, stoned, peeled and chopped

125 g/4½ oz natural yogurt

1 Preheat the oven to 180°C/350°F/Gas Mark 4.

2 Mix the oats and honey together in a bowl and spread out on a baking sheet. Bake in the preheated oven for 10–15 minutes, stirring a couple of times, until the oats are lightly browned, then remove from the oven and leave to cool.

3 Place the seeds in a mortar and briefly grind with a pestle to break them into smaller pieces. Mix with the cooled oats and the walnuts.

4 To assemble, put half the chopped pear and half the chopped mango in a glass and top with half the yogurt and a spoonful of oat mixture. Repeat with the remaining fruit and yogurt and top with more oat mixture.

Bircher Muesli

INGREDIENTS

serves 4

250 g/9 oz rolled oats

1 tbsp wheatgerm

200 ml/7 fl oz full-fat milk or soya milk

2 tbsp clear honey, plus extra for serving (optional)

2 tbsp natural yogurt

1 apple, peeled, cored and grated

150 g/5½ oz chopped nuts, such as macadamia nuts, cashew nuts or hazelnuts

mixed berries, such as blueberries, raspberries and strawberries

fruit purée, to serve (optional)

1 The night before serving, mix the oats, wheatgerm and milk together in a bowl, cover with clingfilm and chill overnight.

2 To serve, stir the oat mixture, add the honey, if using, yogurt and apple, and mix well.

3 Spoon into serving bowls, top with the nuts and berries and drizzle over a little more honey, or fruit purée, if using.

Apple & Hazelnut Bread

INGREDIENTS

makes 1 loaf

butter, for greasing

350 ml/12 fl oz warm water

1 tsp golden caster sugar

1 x 7-g/¼-oz sachet easy-blend dried yeast

400 g/14 oz plain white flour, plus extra for dusting

400 g/14 oz light brown self-raising flour

½ tsp sea salt

125 g/4½ oz toasted hazelnuts, chopped

50 g/1¾ oz dried apple, chopped

1 eating apple, grated

honey and sliced banana or nut butter, to serve

1 Grease and line a 450-g/1-lb loaf tin. Put 100 ml/3½ fl oz of the warm water in a jug, stir in the sugar and yeast and leave for 15 minutes.

2 Mix the flours, salt, nuts, dried apple and fresh apple together in a large bowl. Make a well in the centre, pour in the yeast mixture and gradually work into the flour mixture. Mix in the remaining warm water and bring together to form a soft dough.

3 Turn out onto a floured work surface and knead briefly. Shape the dough into a rectangle and place in the prepared tin. Cover with a warm, damp cloth and set aside in a warm place for 40 minutes until the dough has risen.

4 Meanwhile, preheat the oven to 200°C/400°F/Gas Mark 6. Remove the cloth and bake the loaf in the preheated oven for 40 minutes. Carefully lift out of the tin and return the loaf to the oven, upside down, for 10–15 minutes – the loaf should sound hollow when tapped on the bottom.

5 Remove from the oven and leave to cool on a wire rack. Slice and serve spread with honey, and sliced banana or nut butter. Store wrapped in foil for up to three days, or freeze for up to a month.

Baked Egg with Ham & Tomato

INGREDIENTS

serves 1

1 tsp olive oil

½ small leek, chopped

2 slices wafer-thin ham, chopped

1 egg

25 g/1 oz Cheddar cheese, grated

2 slices tomato

1 Preheat the oven to 180°C/350°F/Gas Mark 4. Heat the oil in a saucepan and cook the leek for 5–6 minutes until soft.

2 Place the leek in the bottom of a ramekin and top with the ham. Crack and pour in the egg, then top with the cheese and tomato.

3 Bake in the preheated oven for 10 minutes until the egg is set. Remove the ramekin from the oven, leave to cool a little, wrap in a cloth and serve.

Waffles with Caramelized Banana

INGREDIENTS

makes 12 waffles to serve 4–6

175 g/6 oz plain flour

2 tsp baking powder

½ tsp salt

2 tsp caster sugar

2 eggs, separated

250 ml/9 fl oz milk

85 g/3 oz butter, melted

100 g/3½ oz butter, cut into pieces

3 tbsp golden syrup

3 large ripe bananas, peeled and thickly sliced

1 Mix the flour, baking powder, salt and sugar together in a bowl. Whisk the egg yolks, milk and melted butter together with a fork, then stir this mixture into the dry ingredients to make a smooth batter.

2 Using an electric mixer or hand whisk, whisk the egg whites in a clean bowl until stiff peaks form. Fold into the batter mixture. Spoon 2 large tablespoons of the batter into a preheated waffle maker and cook according to the manufacturer's instructions.

3 To make the caramelized bananas, melt the butter with the golden syrup in a saucepan over a low heat and stir until combined. Leave to simmer for a few minutes until the caramel thickens and darkens slightly. Add the bananas and mix gently to coat. Pour over the warm waffles and serve immediately.

Fruity Maple Oatmeal

INGREDIENTS

serves 1

175 ml/6 fl oz milk or soya milk, plus extra to serve (optional)

50 g/1¾ oz porridge oats

1 tbsp maple syrup or clear honey

mixed fresh fruit, such as apples,pears, bananas, peaches, mangoes, strawberries and raspberries, prepared and chopped

1 Mix the milk and oats together in a saucepan and cook over a medium heat, stirring, for 8–10 minutes.

2 Serve drizzled with the maple syrup and topped with the fresh fruit, with a little more milk if needed.

3 To make a breakfast brûlée, preheat the grill and put the chopped fruit in the bottom of a ramekin. Top with the cooked porridge and a spoonful of brown sugar and place under the grill until the sugar has melted and caramelized. Chill before serving.

2 Meat & Poultry

The recipes in this chapter can be enjoyed by adults and children alike. Pasta with meat sauce or tasty mini meatballs is a universal favourite, as are meat pie with a creamy potato topping, and finger-licking sticky drumsticks. There are exciting ideas from around the world too. Older children will love the tasty flavours of sweet-and-sour chicken, fragrant Moroccan couscous or mildly spicy Mexican-style roll-ups and quesadillas.

Mini Meatballs & Spaghetti

INGREDIENTS

55 g/2 oz lean beef mince

1 tsp finely chopped onion

2 tsp chopped fresh basil

1 tbsp home-made fresh wholemeal breadcrumbs

1 tsp olive oil

100 ml/3½ fl oz ready-made organic tomato sauce

55 g/2 oz dried spaghetti, broken into short lengths

finely chopped fresh parsley (optional)

makes 8–10 meatballs

1 To make the meatballs, put the mince, onion, basil and breadcrumbs into a small bowl and process using a hand blender. Divide and shape the mixture into even bite-sized balls.

2 Heat the oil in a small saucepan and fry the meatballs, turning frequently, for 2–3 minutes, until lightly browned. Pour over the sauce, cover and simmer gently for about 10 minutes.

3 Cook the spaghetti in a separate saucepan according to the packet instructions. Drain. Serve the spaghetti topped with the meatballs and sauce. Sprinkle with parsley, if using.

Spaghetti Bolognese

INGREDIENTS

serves 4

350 g/12 oz spaghetti or pasta of your choice

grated Parmesan cheese, for sprinkling (optional)

BOLOGNESE SAUCE

2 tbsp olive oil

1 onion, finely chopped

2 garlic cloves, finely chopped

1 carrot, peeled and finely chopped

85 g/3 oz mushrooms, peeled and sliced or chopped (optional)

1 tsp dried oregano

½ tsp dried thyme

1 bay leaf

280 g/10 oz lean beef mince

300 ml/10 fl oz stock

300 ml/10 fl oz passata

pepper

1 To make the sauce, heat the oil in a heavy-based, non-stick saucepan. Add the onion and sauté, half covered, for 5 minutes, or until soft. Add the garlic, carrot and mushrooms, if using, and sauté for a further 3 minutes, stirring occasionally.

2 Add the herbs and mince to the pan and cook until the meat has browned, stirring regularly.

3 Add the stock and passata. Reduce the heat, season to taste and cook over a medium–low heat, half covered, for 15–20 minutes, or until the sauce has reduced and thickened. Remove the bay leaf.

4 Meanwhile, cook the pasta according to the instructions on the packet, until the pasta is tender. Drain well and mix together the pasta and sauce until the pasta is well coated. Serve immediately, sprinkled with the grated Parmesan cheese, if using.

Brilliant Burgers

INGREDIENTS

makes 4–6

450 g beef mince

1 onion, finely chopped

1 egg, beaten

salt and freshly ground black pepper

1 tbsp flour for shaping

1 tbsp olive oil

TO SERVE

4–6 burger buns

½ lettuce

2 tomatoes

mustard, ketchup or mayonnaise

1 Put the mince in the mixing bowl and add the onion, egg and seasoning. Mix well.

2 Lightly flour your hands and the chopping board. Divide the mixture into 4–6 equal portions and shape into burgers.

3 Chill the burgers in the fridge for 10 minutes. Preheat the grill. Place the chilled burgers on the grill pan and brush with oil.

4 Grill the burgers for 4–6 minutes. Turn the burgers over and brush again with oil. Grill for a further 4–6 minutes until done.

5 Cut the buns in half. Toast them under the hot grill if you wish. Slice the tomatoes thinly. Wash and shred the lettuce.

6 Place a handful of lettuce in each bun, then add the burger and a slice of tomato. Serve with your own choice of sauce.

Shepherd's Pie

INGREDIENTS

serves 4

2 tbsp olive oil

750 g/1 lb 10 oz lean fresh lamb mince

1 leek, chopped

1 small red onion, finely chopped

2 carrots, chopped

1 celery stick, chopped

100 g/3½ oz mushrooms, chopped

400 g/14 oz canned tomatoes

2 tbsp fresh thyme leaves

125 ml/4 fl oz water

500 g/1 lb 2 oz potatoes, boiled and mashed

400 g/14 oz sweet potatoes, boiled and mashed

4 tbsp milk

knob of unsalted butter

salt and pepper

1 Heat half the oil in a non-stick frying pan and cook the mince over a high heat, breaking it up with a wooden spoon, until well browned. Remove the mince from the pan with a slotted spoon, pour away any fat and wipe the pan with kitchen paper.

2 Add the remaining oil to the frying pan and cook the leek, onion, carrots and celery for 15 minutes until soft. Return the mince to the pan and add the mushrooms, tomatoes, thyme and water. Season to taste with salt and pepper and leave to simmer for 40 minutes, stirring occasionally.

3 Meanwhile, preheat the oven to 180°C/350°F/Gas Mark 4. Mix the 2 mashes of potatoes with half the milk and half the butter in a bowl and season to taste with salt and pepper.

4 Spoon the meat sauce into a baking dish and top with the potato mixture. Brush with the remaining milk and dot with the remaining butter. Bake in the preheated oven for 35 minutes until the topping is brown and crisp.

Ham Pizza

INGREDIENTS

serves 4

BASE

225 g/8 oz strong white flour

½ tsp salt

2 tsp easy-blend yeast

1 tbsp vegetable oil

175 ml/6 fl oz warm water

2 tbsp flour for dusting

TOPPING

400 g/14 oz canned chopped tomatoes

2 tbsp tomato purée

2 tsp dried oregano

salt and pepper

2 slices of ham, torn into bite-sized pieces

150 g/5½ oz mozzarella cheese, torn into bite-sized pieces

1 yellow pepper, sliced

4 button mushrooms, sliced

2 tbsp olive oil

1 Mix the flour, salt and yeast in a bowl, then add the oil and water. Stir to form a soft dough. Knead the dough on a lightly floured surface until smooth and elastic. Place back in the bowl, cover and leave in a warm place for an hour.

2 Once the dough has risen, flour your hands and the work surface. Knead the dough until smooth. Stretch into shape and roll thinly into two circles, 15 cm across.

3 Pinch up the edges of the dough. Grease the baking sheets. Place the bases on the sheets and leave them to rise while you make the topping.

4 Preheat the oven to 220°C/425°F/Gas Mark 7. Drain the tomatoes and put into a bowl with the tomato purée and oregano. Mix and season.

5 Spread half the mixture over each base. Arrange the ham, cheese, pepper and mushrooms on top. Brush over the olive oil.

6 Bake in the oven for 15–20 minutes until the crusts are pale golden and firm. Remove from the oven and serve.

Perfect Pasta

INGREDIENTS

serves 4

250 g/9 oz pasta shapes

¼ tsp salt

55 g/2 oz butter

40 g/1½ oz plain flour

450 ml/16 fl oz milk

125 g/4½ oz Cheddar cheese, grated

125 g/4½ oz cooked ham, roughly chopped

4 cherry tomatoes, cut into quarters

grated Parmesan cheese, for sprinkling

1 Preheat the oven to 200°C/400°F/Gas Mark 6. Heat some water in the large saucepan. Add salt and bring to the boil.

2 Add the pasta carefully, taking care not to splash. Cook the pasta according to the pack instructions.

3 Gently melt the butter in a saucepan over a low heat. Add the flour and mix well. Cook the mixture for 1 minute, then remove from heat.

4 Stir in the milk, a little at a time, to make a smooth sauce. Put the pan back on the heat. Stir while the sauce thickens so it doesn't go lumpy.

5 When the sauce boils, reduce the heat and cook, stirring, for 1–2 minutes. Remove from heat. Mix in the Cheddar cheese, ham and tomatoes. Season.

6 Drain the pasta. Mix with the sauce. Place in an ovenproof dish and sprinkle with the Parmesan cheese. Bake in the preheated oven, on a baking tray, for 20–25 minutes.

Home-Made Chicken Nuggets

INGREDIENTS

3 skinless, boneless chicken breasts

60 g/2¼ oz wholemeal plain flour

1 tbsp wheatgerm

½ tsp ground cumin

½ tsp ground coriander

1 egg, lightly beaten

2 tbsp olive oil

pepper

DIPPING SAUCE

100 g/3½ oz sunblush tomatoes

100 g/3½ oz fresh tomatoes, peeled, deseeded and chopped

2 tbsp mayonnaise

serves 4

1 Preheat the oven to 190°C/375°F/Gas Mark 5. Cut the chicken breasts into 4-cm/1½-inch chunks. Mix the flour, wheatgerm, cumin, coriander, and pepper to taste, in a bowl, then divide in half and put on 2 separate plates. Put the beaten egg on a third plate.

2 Pour the oil into a baking tray and heat in the oven. Roll the chicken pieces in one plate of flour, shake to remove any excess, then roll in the egg and finally in the second plate of flour, again shaking off any excess flour. When all the nuggets are ready, remove the baking tray from the oven and toss the nuggets in the hot oil. Roast in the oven for 25–30 minutes until golden and crisp.

3 Meanwhile, to make the dipping sauce, put both kinds of tomatoes in a blender or food processor and process until smooth. Add the mayonnaise and process again until well combined.

4 Remove the nuggets from the oven and drain on kitchen paper. Serve with the dipping sauce.

Chicken & Apple Bites

INGREDIENTS

makes 24

1 apple, peeled, cored and grated

2 skinless, boneless chicken breasts, cut into chunks

½ red onion, finely chopped

1 tbsp finely chopped fresh parsley

50 g/1¾ oz fresh wholemeal breadcrumbs

1 tbsp concentrated chicken stock

wholemeal flour, for coating

groundnut oil, for shallow-frying

1 Spread the apple out on a clean tea towel and press out all the excess moisture.

2 Put the chicken, apple, onion, parsley, breadcrumbs and stock in a food processor and pulse briefly until well combined.

3 Spread the flour out on a plate. Divide the mixture into 20 mini portions, shape each portion into a ball and roll in the flour.

4 Heat a little oil in a non-stick frying pan over a medium heat and cook the balls for 5–8 minutes, or until golden brown all over and cooked through. Remove and drain on kitchen paper. Serve hot or cold.

Chicken Skewers

INGREDIENTS

serves 4

4 skinless chicken breasts, about 140 g/5 oz each

2 tbsp extra virgin olive oil

2 tbsp lemon juice

SATAY SAUCE

125 g/4½ oz smooth no-sugar peanut butter

1½ tbsp olive oil

2 tbsp hot water

1½ tbsp light soy sauce

2 tbsp fresh apple juice

4 tbsp coconut milk

1 To make the sauce, mix all the ingredients together in a serving bowl.

2 Soak 16 wooden skewers in water for at least 30 minutes to prevent them burning. Cut each chicken breast lengthways into 4 strips and thread each strip onto a skewer.

3 Mix the oil and lemon juice together in a small bowl, then brush over the chicken.

4 Preheat a griddle pan or grill to medium–high. Cook the chicken skewers, in batches, for 3 minutes on each side, or until golden and cooked through, making sure that there is no trace of pink inside. Keep the cooked chicken skewers warm while cooking the remaining skewers. Serve the skewers with the sauce.

Sweet & Sour Chicken Stir-Fry

INGREDIENTS

serves 2

55 g/2 oz medium egg noodles

1 tbsp vegetable oil

55 g/2 oz skinless, boneless chicken breast, cut into thin strips

½ small carrot, cut into matchsticks

2 baby sweetcorn, halved widthways and lengthways

4 mangetout, cut into strips

55 g/2 oz pineapple, chopped

2 spring onions, sliced

25 g/1 oz pak choi or baby spinach, roughly torn

1 tsp pineapple juice

1 tsp light soy sauce

1 tsp rice or sherry vinegar

soy sauce (optional) and sweet chilli sauce (optional), to serve

1 Cook or soak the noodles according to the packet instructions. Heat the oil in a wok and stir-fry the chicken until lightly browned and cooked through. Add the carrot, baby sweetcorn, mangetout, pineapple and spring onions and cook for 1–2 minutes. Add the pak choi, pineapple juice, soy sauce and vinegar and stir together until the pak choi has just wilted.

2 Drain the noodles and serve topped with the chicken and vegetables. Add a little more soy sauce if using; older children may like a little sweet chilli sauce with this.

Chicken Quesadilla Triangles

INGREDIENTS

serves 1–2

2 small (20-cm/8-inch) flour tortillas

1–2 tsp melted butter, for brushing

½ small cooked skinless, boneless chicken breast, finely chopped

85 g/3 oz grated Cheddar cheese (or a mixture of Cheddar cheese and mozzarella cheese)

1 tomato, skinned, deseeded and diced

2 tsp soured cream flavoured with a squeeze of lime juice and a little chopped coriander, to serve

1 Preheat the oven to 200°C/400°F/Gas Mark 6.

2 Lightly brush one tortilla with a little melted butter and place, buttered side down, on a baking sheet. Arrange the chicken, cheese and tomato over the tortilla, leaving a gap around the edge.

3 Place the second tortilla on top and brush with the remaining butter. Bake for about 10 minutes until the cheese has melted and the top is brown. Allow to cool slightly then cut into triangles and serve with the soured cream.

Tex-Mex Roll-Ups

INGREDIENTS

serves 2

2 corn tortillas

2 tbsp with canned organic baked beans, mashed

2 tbsp grated Cheddar cheese

2–3 tbsp cooked chicken, finely chopped or shredded

1 tomato, sliced

¼ avocado, peeled and cut into strips

1 Put each tortilla on a microwaveable plate. Spread the beans over each tortilla and sprinkle with the cheese. Microwave on HIGH, for about 15 seconds until the cheese melts. Cool slightly. Arrange the chicken, tomato and avocado on top. Roll up and cut into small pieces.

Sticky Drumsticks & Cucumber Salad

INGREDIENTS

serves 6

6 chicken drumsticks

2 tbsp maple syrup

2 tbsp low-salt soy sauce

1 tsp sesame oil

½ cucumber, thinly sliced

2 spring onions, thinly sliced

salt

1 Preheat the oven to 190°C/375°F/Gas Mark 5. Trim the chicken drumsticks of any excess skin and pat dry with kitchen paper.

2 Mix the maple syrup, soy sauce and sesame oil in a large bowl. Add the chicken drumsticks and toss well to coat.

3 Place the chicken drumsticks on a non-stick baking sheet and roast in the preheated oven for 30–40 minutes, basting occasionally, until the chicken is tender, well browned and sticky, and the juices run clear when a skewer is inserted into the thickest part of the meat.

4 Meanwhile, put the cucumber in a colander and sprinkle with a little salt. Leave for 10 minutes until the juices have drained out. Pat dry with kitchen paper and mix with the spring onions.

5 Serve the chicken hot or cold with the cucumber salad.

3 Fish & Seafood

It often seems an easy option to choose ready-made fish fingers or fish cakes, but what could be more satisfying than preparing your own? Children love them made with flavoursome fish such as salmon or tuna. Pasta mixed with tiny nuggets of fish is easy to eat and never fails to please – even the fussiest eater will be clamouring for seconds. Fish and rice is another foolproof option – mixed with eggs it is particularly delicious and healthy too.

Tuna & Pasta Salad

INGREDIENTS

serves 2

100 g/3½ oz small wholewheat pasta shapes

2 tbsp olive oil, plus extra if needed

1 tbsp mayonnaise

1 tbsp natural yogurt

2 tbsp pesto

200 g/7 oz canned tuna in spring water, drained and flaked

200 g/7 oz canned no-added-sugar sweetcorn kernels, drained

2 tomatoes, peeled, deseeded and chopped

½ green pepper, deseeded and chopped

½ avocado, stoned, peeled and chopped

salt and pepper

1 Bring a large saucepan of lightly salted water to the boil, add the pasta and cook for 8–10 minutes, until just tender. Drain, return to the saucepan and add half the oil. Toss well to coat, then cover and leave to cool.

2 Whisk the mayonnaise, yogurt and pesto together in a jug, adding a little oil if needed to achieve the desired consistency. Acd a pinch of salt and season to taste with pepper.

3 Mix the pasta with the tuna, sweetcorn, tomatoes, green pepper and avocado, add the dressing and toss well to coat.

Tortillas with Tuna, Egg & Sweetcorn

INGREDIENTS

serves 2

1 large egg, hard-boiled and cooled

200 g/7 oz canned tuna in spring water, drained

200 g/7 oz canned no-added-sugar sweetcorn kernels, drained

2 wholemeal flour tortillas

1 punnet mustard cress

DRESSING

1 tbsp natural yogurt

1 tsp olive oil

½ tsp white wine vinegar

½ tsp Dijon mustard

pepper

1 To make the dressing, whisk the yogurt, oil, vinegar, mustard, and pepper to taste in a jug until emulsified and smooth.

2 Shell the egg, separate the yolk and the white, then mash the yolk and chop the white finely. Mash the tuna with the egg and dressing, then mix in the sweetcorn.

3 Spread the filling equally over the 2 tortillas and sprinkle over the mustard cress. Fold in one end of each tortilla and roll up.

Tuna Bites

INGREDIENTS

makes 24

200 g/7 oz canned tuna in spring water, drained

1 egg

1 tsp finely chopped fresh parsley

50 g/1¾ oz fresh wholemeal breadcrumbs

about 1 tbsp wholemeal plain flour

vegetable oil, for brushing

salt and pepper

1 Mash the tuna with the egg, parsley, a pinch of salt, and pepper to taste. Add the breadcrumbs and mix well, then add enough of the flour to bind the mixture together.

2 Divide the mixture into 20 mini portions, shape each portion into a ball and chill for 15 minutes.

3 Meanwhile, preheat the oven to 190°C/375°F/Gas Mark 5. Brush a non-stick baking sheet with a little oil. Space the tuna balls out on the baking sheet and brush with a little more oil. Bake in the preheated oven for 15–20 minutes until golden and crisp.

4 Remove from the oven and drain on kitchen paper. Serve warm or cold.

Home-Made Fish Fingers & Sweet Potato Wedges

INGREDIENTS

makes 8–10

280 g/10 oz thick cod fillets, skin and bones removed

flour, for dusting

1 tsp paprika

fresh breadcrumbs or fine cornmeal, for coating

1 egg, beaten

sunflower oil, for frying

fresh or frozen peas, cooked, to serve

SWEET POTATO WEDGES

450 g/1 lb sweet potatoes, scrubbed and cut into wedges

1 tbsp olive oil

salt and pepper

1 To make the potato wedges, preheat the oven to 200°C/400°F/Gas Mark 6. Dry the sweet potato wedges on a clean tea towel. Place the oil in a roasting tin and heat for a few minutes in the oven. Arrange the potatoes in the tin and bake for 30–35 minutes, turning them halfway through, until tender and golden.

2 Meanwhile, cut the cod into strips about 2-cm/¾-inch wide. Put the flour onto a plate, add the paprika and season to taste. Put the breadcrumbs onto a second plate. Roll the cod strips in the seasoned flour until coated, shaking off any excess, then dip them in the beaten egg. Roll the cod strips in the breadcrumbs until evenly coated.

3 Heat enough oil to cover the base of a large, non-stick frying pan. Carefully arrange the fish fingers in the pan – you may have to cook them in batches – and fry them for 3–4 minutes on each side or until crisp and golden. Drain on kitchen paper before serving, if necessary.

4 Serve the fish fingers with the sweet potato wedges and peas.

Two-Fish Casserole

INGREDIENTS

serves 4–6

85 g/3 oz dried penne or macaroni

2 tsp olive oil, plus extra for coating pasta

1 egg

1 small onion, finely chopped

1 small celery stick, finely chopped

1 small carrot, peeled and finely chopped

small handful of spinach leaves, tough stalks removed and finely shredded

120 ml/4 fl oz milk

2 tbsp double cream

25 g/1 oz mature Cheddar cheese, grated

½ tsp English mustard

1 tbsp finely chopped fresh parsley

squeeze of fresh lemon juice

90 g/3¼ oz undyed smoked haddock, skinned and boned

140 g/5 oz white fish, skinned and boned

85 g/3 oz mozzarella cheese, diced

1 Preheat the oven to 200°C/400°F/Gas Mark 6. Cook the pasta according to the instructions on the packet, until tender. Drain well. Toss in oil.

2 Bring a small saucepan of water to the boil and add the egg. Cook for 8–10 minutes, until the egg is hard boiled. Cool the egg under cold running water.

3 Heat the oil in a heavy-based frying pan. Add the onion and sauté for 5 minutes, until softened, then add the celery and carrot and sauté for 3 minutes. Add the spinach and cook for a further 2 minutes, until tender.

4 Stir in the milk and cream and bring to the boil. Turn off the heat and stir in the Cheddar cheese, mustard, parsley and lemon juice.

5 Place the fish in a small ovenproof dish. Shell and chop the hard-boiled egg and spoon it over the fish, then top with the sauce. Arrange the pasta over the top and sprinkle with the mozzarella cheese. Bake for 20–25 minutes, until brown on top.

Salmon Cakes

INGREDIENTS

700 g/1 lb 9 oz skinless salmon fillet, cut into cubes

300 ml/10 fl oz milk

1 bay leaf

100 g/3½ oz broccoli, steamed until tender

700 g/1 lb 9 oz potatoes, boiled and mashed

2 tbsp finely chopped fresh parsley

4 tbsp wholemeal plain flour

1 egg yolk

2 large eggs, beaten

150 g/5½ oz fresh wholemeal breadcrumbs

2 tbsp olive oil

pepper

makes ❶❷

1 Preheat the oven to 200°C/400°F/Gas Mark 6. Put the salmon in a saucepan with the milk and bay leaf and bring slowly up to simmering point. Simmer for 2 minutes, then remove the pan from the heat, lift out and discard the bay leaf and leave the fish in the milk to cool. When cool, lift out the fish with a slotted spoon and place on kitchen paper to drain.

2 Flake the fish into a large bowl. Put the broccoli in a food processor and pulse until smooth. Add to the fish with the mashed potatoes, the parsley, 1 tablespoon of the flour, and pepper to taste. Add the egg yolk and mix well. If the mixture is a little dry, add some of the poaching milk; if too wet, add a little more flour.

3 Divide the mixture into 12 portions and shape each portion into a cake. Put the beaten eggs, the remaining flour and the breadcrumbs on 3 separate plates. Roll each fishcake in the flour, then in the beaten egg, and then in the breadcrumbs to coat.

4 Heat the oil in a non-stick baking tray in the preheated oven for 5 minutes. Add the fish cakes and bake for 10 minutes, then carefully turn the fish cakes over and bake for a further 10 minutes.

Salmon with Egg-Fried Rice

INGREDIENTS

200 g/7 oz skinless salmon fillet

2 tsp clear honey

1 tbsp light soy sauce

3 tsp vegetable oil

1 small carrot, finely chopped

2 tbsp frozen peas

½ red pepper, deseeded and chopped

1 egg, beaten

85 g/3 oz basmati rice, cooked

1 spring onion, finely sliced

lightly cooked spinach or pak choi, to serve

serves 2

1 Cut the salmon into 2 pieces and place in a shallow dish. Mix together the honey and soy sauce and brush over the salmon. Leave for 10 minutes.

2 Heat 2 teaspoons of the oil and cook the carrot for about 5 minutes. Add the peas and pepper and cook for a further 5 minutes until soft. Add the beaten egg and cook over a gentle heat, stirring and breaking up the egg into little pieces. Add the cooked rice and heat through for a few minutes.

3 Heat the remaining oil in a small frying pan and cook the salmon for 2–3 minutes on each side. Alternatively, cook the fish under the grill. Stir the spring onion into the rice. Serve the salmon on a bed of spinach accompanied by the egg-fried rice.

Creamy Smoked Salmon & Broccoli Pasta

INGREDIENTS

serves 4

400 g/14 oz pasta shells, bows or tagliatelle

225 g/8 oz broccoli florets

1 tbsp olive oil

2 tbsp butter

1 leek, finely chopped

200 g/7 oz tub garlic and herb cream cheese

6 tbsp whole milk

100 g/3½ oz smoked salmon pieces

salt and pepper

1 Cook the pasta according to the instructions on the packet, until the pasta is tender, then drain. Meanwhile, steam the broccoli for 8–10 minutes, or until tender.

2 At the same time, prepare the sauce. Heat the oil and butter in a small heavy-based frying pan, then add the leek and sauté for 7 minutes, or until softened. Gently stir in the cream cheese and milk and heat through.

3 Add the smoked salmon pieces and cook for a minute or so, until they turn opaque. Combine the sauce with the pasta and broccoli and mix together well. Season to taste.

Honey Salmon Kebabs

INGREDIENTS

serves 2

4 boneless salmon fillets, each about 140 g/5 oz, skinned and cut into 2-cm/¾-in cubes

1 tbsp toasted sesame seeds (optional)

cooked rice, to serve

MARINADE

2 tbsp clear honey

1 tbsp soy sauce

1 tbsp olive oil

1 tsp toasted sesame oil

1 Mix together the ingredients for the marinade in a shallow dish. Add the salmon and stir to coat the fish in the marinade. Leave to marinate in the refrigerator for 1 hour, turning the fish occasionally.

2 Preheat the grill to high. Thread the cubes of salmon onto 4–6 skewers. Line a grill rack with foil and place the skewers on top. Brush the salmon with the marinade and grill for 3–5 minutes, turning the skewers occasionally, until cooked.

3 While the salmon is cooking, put the remaining marinade in a small saucepan and heat for a few minutes until it has reduced and thickened.

4 Serve the kebabs with rice. Spoon the reduced marinade over the salmon and sprinkle with sesame seeds, if using.

Fish Pie

INGREDIENTS

1 tbsp olive oil

1 onion, finely chopped

1 celery stick, finely chopped

1 carrot, peeled and finely chopped

small handful of spinach leaves, tough stalks removed and finely shredded

250 ml/8 fl oz full-cream milk

4 tbsp double cream

55 g/2 oz mature Cheddar cheese, grated

1 tsp Dijon mustard

2 tbsp finely chopped fresh parsley

squeeze of fresh lemon juice

225 g/8 oz undyed smoked haddock, skin and bones removed, cut into pieces

225 g/8 oz cod fillet, skin and bones removed

2 hard-boiled eggs

1 sheet of ready-rolled puff pastry, defrosted if using frozen

1 egg, beaten, to glaze

salt and pepper

serves 4

1 Preheat the oven to 200°C/400°F/Gas Mark 6.

2 Heat the oil in a heavy-based frying pan. Add the onion and sauté for 5 minutes, or until softened, then add the celery and carrot and sauté for 3 minutes. Add the spinach and cook for a further 2 minutes, or until tender.

3 Stir in the milk and cream and bring to the boil. Turn off the heat and stir in the Cheddar cheese, mustard, parsley and lemon juice. Season to taste.

4 Place the fish in an ovenproof dish. Peel and chop the egg and spoon it over the fish, then top with the creamy vegetable sauce.

5 Place the pastry on a lightly floured work surface. Make fish and starfish shapes using biscuit cutters, then arrange them on top of the fish pie. Brush the pastry shapes with beaten egg and bake for 20–25 minutes, or until the fish is cooked and the pastry shapes have risen and are a golden brown colour.

Sunny Rice

INGREDIENTS

serves 4

450 g/1 lb undyed smoked haddock or cod fillets

milk, for poaching

225 g/8 oz basmati rice, rinsed

450 ml/16 fl oz water

1 bay leaf

2 cloves

4 tbsp butter

55 g/2 oz frozen petit pois

1 tsp garam masala

½ tsp ground turmeric

2 tbsp chopped flat-leaf parsley

4 hard-boiled eggs, quartered

pepper

1 Put the haddock in a large frying pan and pour enough milk over the fish to just cover it. Poach the fish for 5 minutes, or until cooked and opaque. Remove the haddock from the pan and flake the fish, carefully removing the skin and any bones. Discard the remainder of the poaching liquid.

2 Meanwhile, place the rice in a saucepan and cover with the water, then add the bay leaf and cloves. Bring to the boil, then reduce the heat and simmer, covered, for 15 minutes, or until the water has been absorbed and the rice is tender. Discard the bay leaf and cloves. Set aside the covered pan.

3 Melt the butter over a gentle heat in the cleaned frying pan, then add the peas and cook for 2 minutes, or until tender. Stir in the garam masala and turmeric and cook for another minute.

4 Stir in the haddock and rice and mix well until they are coated in the spiced butter.

5 Season and heat through for 1–2 minutes. Stir in the parsley and top with the hard-boiled eggs just before serving.

Surf 'n' Turf Paella

INGREDIENTS

2 tbsp olive oil

1 onion, diced

2 skinless chicken breasts, sliced

1 small red pepper, deseeded and diced

2 garlic cloves, chopped

1 tomato, deseeded and chopped

1 tbsp tomato purée

pinch of saffron

600 ml/1 pint hot chicken stock or vegetable stock

175 g/6 oz paella rice

55 g/2 oz frozen peas

115 g/4 oz cooked prawns, thawed if frozen

salt and pepper

serves 2–3

1 Heat the oil in a large heavy-based sauté pan (with a lid). Add the onion and fry for 5 minutes, or until soft. Add the chicken, pepper and garlic and sauté for 5 minutes over a medium heat, stirring frequently to prevent the mixture sticking.

2 Add the tomato, tomato purée, saffron and stock to the pan. Stir in the rice and bring to the boil, then reduce the heat and simmer, covered, for 15 minutes or until the rice is tender.

3 Add the peas, prawns and seasoning and cook for a further 2–3 minutes, or until the prawns have heated through.

Prawns with Coconut Rice

INGREDIENTS

115 g/4 oz dried Chinese mushrooms

2 tbsp vegetable or groundnut oil

6 spring onions, chopped

55 g/2 oz desiccated coconut

1 fresh green chilli, deseeded and chopped

225 g/8 oz jasmine rice

150 ml/5 fl oz fish stock

400 ml/14 fl oz coconut milk

350 g/12 oz prawns, cooked and peeled

6 sprigs fresh Thai basil

serves 4

1 Place the mushrooms in a small bowl, cover with hot water and set aside to soak for 30 minutes. Drain, then cut off and discard the stalks and slice the caps.

2 Heat 1 tablespoon of the oil in a wok and stir-fry the spring onions, coconut and chilli for 2–3 minutes, until lightly browned. Add the mushrooms and stir-fry for 3–4 minutes.

3 Add the rice and stir-fry for 2–3 minutes, then add the stock and bring to the boil. Reduce the heat and add the coconut milk. Simmer for 10–15 minutes, until the rice is tender. Stir in the prawns and basil, heat through and serve.

4 Vegetables

Vegetables are vital for health, but getting children to eat them can be a challenge. Try recipes using sweetcorn or carrots – young children love the bright colours. Chopped small or puréed, vegetables are easier to chew and swallow. They can be disguised in nutritious soups or served as part of a dish based on energy-rich foods such as eggs, pasta or beans. Vegetable-based omelettes, lasagne and bean burgers are a hit with children of all ages.

Minestrone Soup

INGREDIENTS

serves 2–4

1 tbsp sunflower oil

2 tbsp chopped onion

1 garlic clove, chopped

½ tsp Italian herb seasoning

25 g/1 oz carrot, chopped

2 tsp very finely chopped celery

25 g/1 oz potato, peeled and chopped

300 ml/10 fl oz unsalted vegetable stock or chicken stock

100 ml/3½ fl oz passata

1 tsp tomato purée

25 g/1 oz dried vermicelli, broken into small pieces

1 tbsp frozen petit pois

10 baby spinach leaves, washed

cheese straws, to serve

1 To make the soup, heat the oil in a small saucepan. Add the onion and cook for a few minutes until soft but not brown. Add the garlic, seasoning, carrot, celery and potato and cook for 1–2 minutes. Stir in the stock, passata and tomato purée.

2 Bring to the boil, add the pasta and peas and then simmer for about 10 minutes, until the vegetables are tender.

3 Stir in the spinach leaves, remove from the heat and cool a little before serving with the cheese straws.

Herby Vegetable & Pasta Cheese

INGREDIENTS

serves 4–6

4 broccoli florets, cut into small florets

4 cauliflower florets, cut into small florets

85 g/3 oz small penne or farfalle pasta

cheese sauce

1½ tbsp unsalted butter or margarine

1 tbsp plain flour

175 ml/6 fl oz full cream milk

½ tsp dried oregano

55 g/2 oz Cheddar cheese, grated

1 Steam the broccoli and cauliflower for 8–10 minutes, until tender. Cook the pasta according to the instructions on the packet, until the pasta is tender, then drain.

2 Meanwhile, make the cheese sauce. Melt the butter in a small heavy-based saucepan over a low heat. Gradually add the flour, beating well to form a smooth paste. Cook for 30 seconds, stirring constantly. Add the milk, a little at a time, whisking well to prevent any lumps forming, then stir in the oregano. Simmer for 2 minutes until smooth and creamy, then mix in the cheese. Stir until melted.

3 Add the cooked vegetables and pasta to the sauce and stir well. Finely chop or mash the mixture, if desired.

Chinese Noodles

INGREDIENTS

serves 4

250 g pack of tofu, drained and cubed

250 g/9 oz medium egg noodles

1 tbsp groundnut oil or vegetable oil

1 red pepper, deseeded and sliced

225 g/8 oz broccoli florets

175 g/6 oz baby sweetcorn, halved lengthways

2–3 tbsp water

2 spring onions, finely sliced

1 tbsp sesame seeds, toasted (optional)

salt

MARINADE

1 garlic clove, finely chopped

2.5-cm/1-inch piece fresh ginger, peeled and grated

1 tsp sesame oil

1 tbsp clear honey

2 tbsp dark soy sauce

1 Mix together the ingredients for the marinade in a shallow dish. Add the tofu and spoon the marinade over. Refrigerate for 1 hour to marinate, turning the tofu occasionally to allow the flavours to infuse.

2 Preheat the oven to 200°C/400°F/Gas Mark 6. Using a slotted spoon, remove the tofu from the marinade and reserve the liquid. Arrange the tofu on a baking sheet and roast for 20 minutes, turning occasionally, until the tofu pieces are golden and crisp on all sides.

3 Meanwhile, cook the noodles according to the instructions on the packet, until tender, then drain. Rinse the noodles under cold running water and drain again.

4 Heat a wok or heavy-based frying pan, then add the oil. Add the pepper, broccoli and sweetcorn and stir-fry, tossing and stirring constantly, over a medium–high heat for 5–8 minutes or until the vegetables have softened. Add the water and continue to stir-fry until the vegetables are just tender but remain slightly crunchy.

5 Stir in the marinade, noodles, tofu and spring onions and stir-fry until heated through. Serve sprinkled with sesame seeds, if using.

Vegetable Lasagne

INGREDIENTS

makes 3–4 invidual lasagne

1 tbsp olive oil

1 red onion, chopped

1 garlic clove, crushed and chopped

100 g/3½ oz courgettes, sliced

100 g/3½ oz baby spinach, washed and roughly torn

250 g/9 oz ricotta cheese

3–4 sheets fresh lasagne

400 ml/14 fl oz ready-made organic tomato sauce

1 quantity Cheese Sauce (see page 114)

100 g/3½ oz mozzarella cheese, roughly chopped

55 g/2 oz fresh Parmesan cheese, grated

1 Preheat the oven to 190°C/375°F/Gas Mark 5.

2 Heat the oil in a saucepan, add the onion and garlic and cook very slowly for about 10 minutes until soft. Add the courgettes and cook for 2–3 minutes. Add the spinach and stir until just wilted then remove from the heat. Allow to cool then drain off any liquid.

3 Mix the cooked vegetables with the ricotta cheese. If necessary, blanch the lasagne according to the packet instructions. Cut each lasagne sheet into pieces to fit individual ovenproof dishes about 12 cm/5 inches square. Spoon a little tomato sauce into each dish. Layer the lasagne, ricotta cheese mixture and tomato sauce in each of the dishes. End with a layer of lasagne. Pour cheese sauce over each lasagne and sprinkle with the mozzarella cheese and Parmesan cheese.

4 Bake for about 20–25 minutes until golden brown.

Hearty Bean & Pasta Soup

INGREDIENTS

serves 4

4 tbsp olive oil

1 onion, finely chopped

1 celery stick, chopped

1 carrot, peeled and diced

1 bay leaf

1.2 litres/2 pints low-salt vegetable stock

400 g/14 oz canned chopped tomatoes

175 g/6 oz dried pasta shapes, such as farfalle, shells or twists

400 g/14 oz canned cannellini beans, drained and rinsed

200 g/7 oz spinach or chard, thick stalks removed and shredded

salt and pepper

40 g/1½ oz Parmesan cheese, finely grated, to serve

1 Heat the olive oil in a large, heavy-based saucepan. Add the onion, celery and carrot and cook over a medium heat for 8–10 minutes, stirring occasionally, until the vegetables have softened.

2 Add the bay leaf, stock and chopped tomatoes, then bring to the boil. Reduce the heat, cover and simmer for 15 minutes, or until the vegetables are just tender.

3 Add the pasta and beans, then bring the soup back to the boil and cook for 10 minutes, or until the pasta is just tender. Stir occasionally to prevent the pasta sticking to the base of the pan and burning.

4 Season to taste, add the spinach and cook for a further 2 minutes, or until tender. Serve, sprinkled with Parmesan cheese.

Creamy Tomato Soup

INGREDIENTS

serves 4

1 tbsp butter

½ red onion, minced

1 leek, chopped

1 garlic clove, crushed

1 carrot, peeled and grated

1 potato, peeled and grated

300 ml/10 fl oz low-salt vegetable stock

500 g/1 lb 2 oz ripe tomatoes, peeled, deseeded and chopped

1 tbsp tomato purée

150 ml/5 fl oz milk

salt and pepper

snipped chives, to garnish (optional)

granary rolls, to serve

1 Melt the butter in a large saucepan over a low heat and cook the onion, leek and garlic for 10 minutes, or until very soft but not brown.

2 Add the carrot and potato and cook for 5 minutes. Add the stock and bring up to simmering point.

3 Add the tomatoes and tomato purée and season to taste with salt and pepper. Simmer for 15 minutes until the vegetables are very soft. Add the milk and warm through, then transfer the soup to a blender or food processor and process until very smooth. You can pass the soup through a sieve at this stage, if you like.

4 Return the soup to the rinsed-out pan and reheat gently. Pour into warmed serving bowls and garnish the soup with the snipped chives, if using. Serve with granary rolls.

Warm Pasta Salad

INGREDIENTS

serves 4

5 tbsp olive oil

1 tbsp lemon juice

2 garlic cloves, flattened with the back of a knife and chopped

1 tsp chopped fresh rosemary

2 tsp chopped fresh thyme

1 red onion, cut into 8 wedges

1 red pepper, deseeded and thickly sliced

1 yellow pepper, deseeded and thickly sliced

4 small courgettes, quartered lengthways

4 plum tomatoes, quartered

250 g/9 oz penne pasta

1 tbsp white wine vinegar

1 tbsp pesto

200 g/7 oz feta cheese, crumbled

handful baby rocket leaves

1 Preheat the oven to 200°C/400°F/Gas Mark 6.

2 Put 2 tablespoons of oil, the lemon juice, garlic and herbs into a large baking tin. Add the onion and peppers and toss in the oil mixture. Cook in the oven for 10–15 minutes. Add the courgettes and tomatoes and cook for a further 10–15 minutes until the vegetables are soft and lightly charred at the edges.

3 Meanwhile, cook the pasta according to the packet instructions. Drain and put into a large bowl. Mix together the remaining oil, the vinegar and pesto, and pour over the pasta. Add the cooled, cooked vegetables and the cheese and toss gently together. Sprinkle over the rocket and serve warm.

Chinese Rice with Omelette Strips

INGREDIENTS

serves 2

2 tsp vegetable oil

few drops of sesame oil

1 small garlic clove, finely chopped

pinch of Chinese five-spice powder

1 carrot, peeled and diced

2 baby sweetcorn, halved and thinly sliced

2 tbsp water

small handful of baby spinach, tough stems removed and finely sliced

175 g/6 oz cold, cooked brown or white rice

dash of soy sauce

1 tsp sesame seeds (optional)

small knob of unsalted butter

1 egg, beaten

1 Heat the vegetable oil and sesame oil in a wok or heavy-based frying pan. Add the garlic, five spice, carrot and sweetcorn and stir-fry for 5 minutes, stirring and tossing constantly to prevent the spices and vegetables burning and sticking.

2 Add the water and stir-fry for 2 minutes, then mix in the spinach and cook, stirring frequently, for a further 2 minutes, or until the vegetables are tender.

3 Add the rice and a splash of soy sauce to the wok or pan and heat through thoroughly. Mix in the sesame seeds, if using.

4 Meanwhile, melt the butter in a small heavy-based frying pan and add the egg. Swirl the egg until it covers the base of the pan. Cook until the egg has set and is cooked through, then turn out onto a plate. Cut the omelette into strips or pieces.

5 Place the rice in a bowl and arrange the omelette in a criss-cross pattern on top.

Cheesy Sweetcorn Fritters

INGREDIENTS

1 egg

200 ml/7 fl oz milk

100 g/3½ oz plain flour

½ tsp baking powder

85 g/3 oz canned sweetcorn kernels without salt or sugar, drained, plus extra to serve

4 tbsp grated Cheddar cheese

1 tsp snipped fresh chives

2 tsp sunflower oil, for frying

mini carrot sticks, to serve

serves 2

1 Put the egg and milk into a small bowl and beat with a fork. Add the flour and baking powder and beat until smooth. Stir in the sweetcorn, cheese and chives. Heat a little sunflower oil in a frying pan and drop either teaspoonfuls or tablespoonfuls of the batter into it. Cook for 1–2 minutes on each side until the fritters are puffed up and golden.

2 Drain on kitchen paper and serve with the extra sweetcorn and mini carrot sticks.

Deep-Pan Omelette

INGREDIENTS

serves 2–4

1 tbsp sunflower oil

½ small onion, chopped

200 g/7 oz waxy potatoes, diced

½ red pepper, deseeded and thinly sliced

1 small courgette, diced

2 tbsp frozen petit pois

1 tbsp chopped fresh parsley

3 eggs, beaten

1 Heat the oil in a 20-cm/8-inch omelette pan. Add the onion and cook for about 5 minutes until soft. Add the potatoes and cook gently for about 10 minutes until just soft. Add the pepper, courgette, petit pois and parsley and cook for 2–3 minutes.

2 Beat the eggs with 1 tablespoon of cold water. Pour over the vegetables in the frying pan. Cook over a very low heat for 5–10 minutes or until the mixture is beginning to set on top and is golden underneath when the edge is lifted with a spatula.

3 Place under a medium grill for 1–2 minutes until the top is set and golden brown. Cool and cut into wedges or strips to serve.

Roast Vegetable Lasagne

INGREDIENTS

serves 4

3 tbsp olive oil

4 courgettes, halved lengthways and thickly sliced

3 red peppers, deseeded and chopped

1 aubergine, chopped

2 red onions, chopped

5 shallots, peeled and quartered

250 g/9 oz button mushrooms

400 g/14 oz canned chopped tomatoes

1 tbsp tomato purée

200 g/7 oz fresh lasagne

2 tbsp grated Parmesan cheese

salt and pepper

CHEESE SAUCE

50 g/1¾ oz butter

50 g/1¾ oz plain flour

600 ml/1 pint milk

100 g/3½ oz Cheddar cheese, grated

1 Preheat the oven to 190°C/375°F/Gas Mark 5. Put the oil in a large bowl, add the courgettes, peppers, aubergine, onions and shallots and toss well to coat.

2 Divide the vegetables between 2 baking trays and roast in the preheated oven for 30–40 minutes until soft and flecked with brown. Add the button mushrooms after 20 minutes.

3 Remove the vegetables from the oven and tip into a large bowl. Add the tomatoes and tomato purée and mix well.

4 Melt the butter in a saucepan over a low heat. Stir in the flour and cook, stirring constantly, for 2–3 minutes. Gradually add the milk and cook, continuing to stir constantly, until the sauce is thick and smooth. Season to taste with salt and pepper and stir in the Cheddar cheese.

5 Layer the vegetable mixture and sauce in an ovenproof dish with the lasagne, finishing with a layer of sauce. Sprinkle over the Parmesan cheese and bake in the oven for 30–35 minutes.

6 Remove from the oven and serve hot.

Bean Burgers

INGREDIENTS

serves 6

400 g/14 oz canned cannellini beans, drained and rinsed

2 tbsp red pesto

75 g/2¾ oz fresh wholemeal breadcrumbs

1 egg

2 tbsp olive oil

½ small red onion, finely chopped

1 garlic clove, crushed

6 granary rolls

6 tsp hummus

salt and pepper

TO SERVE

2 cherry tomatoes, sliced

sliced cucumber

green salad leaves

1 Using a potato masher, mash the beans in a bowl until they are smooth, then add the pesto, breadcrumbs, egg, and a pinch of salt and pepper to taste, and mix well.

2 Heat half the oil in a non-stick frying pan over a low heat and cook the onion and garlic until soft. Add to the bean mixture and mix well.

3 Heat the remaining oil in the frying pan. Spoon in the bean mixture, in 6 separate mounds, then press each one down with the back of a spoon to form a burger.

4 Cook the burgers for 4–5 minutes, then carefully turn over and cook for a further 4–5 minutes, until golden.

5 Meanwhile, slice the rolls in half and smear each one with the hummus.

6 Remove the burgers from the frying pan and drain on kitchen paper. Place each one in a roll, top with the tomatoes, cucumber and salad leaves and serve.

Crispy Vegetable Bake

INGREDIENTS

serves 4

25 g/1 oz butter, plus extra for greasing

750 g/1 lb 10 oz potatoes, thinly sliced

3 tbsp olive oil

1 garlic clove, crushed

1 tsp fresh oregano leaves

1 large leek, shredded

2 parsnips, peeled and grated

3 carrots, peeled and grated

½ head celeriac, peeled and grated

200 g/7 oz feta cheese, crumbled

4 eggs

salt and pepper

1 Preheat the oven to 190°C/375°F/Gas Mark 5. Grease a 20-cm/8-inch round baking dish with butter.

2 Bring a large saucepan of lightly salted water to the boil, add the potatoes and cook for 5 minutes. Drain and cover with a clean tea towel to absorb the steam.

3 Melt half the butter with 1 tablespoon of the oil in a large frying pan and cook the garlic, oregano and leek for 3–4 minutes. Remove with a slotted spoon and transfer to a plate. Add the remaining oil to the frying pan and cook the parsnips, carrots and celeriac for 10 minutes until soft and cooked through. Season to taste with salt and pepper and cook for a further 5 minutes. Stir in the leek mixture.

4 Arrange half the potato slices in the bottom of the prepared dish, top with half the vegetable mixture and then sprinkle over half the cheese. Cover with the remaining vegetable mixture and cheese and top with the remaining potato slices. Dot with the remaining butter and bake in the preheated oven for 40 minutes until golden and crisp.

5 Five minutes before serving, poach the eggs. Serve the vegetable bake topped with the

5 Snacks

Children's appetites are unpredictable but a tasty snack is always welcome, particularly after school when energy levels can be low. This chapter includes sweet and savoury snacks to suit all appetites – from bite-sized sandwiches for babies and toddlers, to hunky cheese on toast for ravenous school children. There are also recipes for healthy finger foods such as dippers, nachos and popcorn that will go down a treat.

Simply Super Sandwich Fillings

INGREDIENTS

serves 3–4

CRUNCHY TUNA

200 g/7 oz canned tuna in spring water, drained and flaked

1 tbsp canned sweetcorn, drained

1 tbsp chopped peppers

1 tbsp mayonnaise

FRUITY CHEESE SPREAD

100 g/3½ oz low-fat soft cheese or ricotta cheese

1 tbsp chopped stoned dates

2 tbsp chopped ready-to-eat dried apricots

CHICKEN & AVOCADO

½ chicken breast, cooked and finely chopped

½ small avocado, mashed with 2 tsp lemon juice

1 Mix the ingredients for the fillings together and store in the refrigerator until required.

Hummus with Crunchy Vegetables

INGREDIENTS

makes 10 portions

200 g/7 oz no-salt, no-sugar canned chickpeas, drained and rinsed

½ garlic clove, crushed

3 tbsp tahini

freshly squeezed lemon juice, to taste

1 tbsp natural yogurt

carrot sticks, red pepper sticks, cucumber sticks and apple wedges, to serve

1 Place the chickpeas in a blender with the garlic, tahini, lemon juice and yogurt. Blend until smooth.

2 Store in the refrigerator for up to 3 days and serve with carrot sticks, red pepper sticks, cucumber sticks and apple wedges.

Grilled Cheese Sandwich

INGREDIENTS

serves 4

1 stoneground buckwheat boule loaf (about 17.5 cm/ 7 inch diameter) or other rustic round loaf

175 g/6 oz Cheddar cheese, finely shaved or coarsely grated

1 large avocado, halved, stoned, peeled and sliced

2 tomatoes, halved and cut into fine wedges

12 freshly cooked asparagus spears

4 slices Parma, serrano or Black Forest ham

olive oil

1 Slice the crusty top off the loaf; reserve for another use. Slice the loaf into two layers, making the bottom layer thicker. Place the bottom on a large piece of foil.

2 Preheat the grill on the hottest setting. Toast the top surface of the top layer of the loaf until brown, then turn it and place on the foil.

3 Sprinkle 100 g/3½ oz of the cheese over both layers of bread. Arrange the avocado and tomato wedges on the bottom layer then sprinkle with half the remaining cheese. Top with the asparagus spears and ham, completely covering the edges of the ingredients underneath. Sprinkle with the remaining cheese and a trickle of olive oil.

4 Place under the grill and cook well away from the heat source for 3–5 minutes. Remove the plain cheese-topped layer first, when the cheese is bubbling. Cook the bottom layer until the cheese has melted and the ham has browned.

5 Cut the toasted cheese layer into 8 wedges and overlap them on the filling, alternating the plain and cheese sides up. Serve at once, cut into four wedges.

Green Fingers

INGREDIENTS

2 soft tortillas

guacamole

½ avocado, stoned and flesh scooped out

½ garlic clove, crushed

squeeze of fresh lemon juice

serves 2

1 Put the avocado, garlic and lemon juice into a bowl. Mash with a fork until fairly smooth and creamy.

2 Warm the tortillas in a large dry frying pan. Spread the guacamole over the tortillas and cut into fingers or wedges, or roll them up.

Cheese Twists

INGREDIENTS

serves 4–6

butter or margarine, for greasing

85 g/3 oz Gruyère cheese, grated

½ tsp paprika

375 g/13 oz ready-rolled puff pastry, defrosted if frozen

1 egg, beaten

1 Preheat the oven to 200°C/400°F/Gas Mark 6. Grease a large baking sheet.

2 Mix together the Gruyère cheese and paprika and sprinkle over the sheet of puff pastry. Fold the puff pastry in half and roll out a little to seal the edges.

3 Cut the pastry into long 1-cm/½-inch wide strips, then cut each strip in half and gently twist. Place on the prepared baking sheet. Brush with the beaten egg and bake for 10–12 minutes, or until crisp and golden. Allow to cool on a wire rack.

Avocado Dip with Spicy Potato Skins

INGREDIENTS

serves 6–8

4 large baking potatoes, scrubbed

3 tbsp olive oil

1 garlic clove, crushed

¼ tsp paprika

½ tsp dried chilli flakes (optional)

AVOCADO DIP

2 ripe avocados, stoned and peeled

juice of ½ lemon

150 g/5½ oz soft goat's cheese

salt and pepper

1 Preheat the oven to 190°C/375°F/Gas Mark 5. Rub the potatoes with 1 tablespoon of the oil, place on a baking sheet and bake in the preheated oven for 1–1½ hours, or until the flesh is soft.

2 Remove the potatoes from the oven, cut in half lengthways and carefully scoop out the flesh into a bowl, but leave a generous 1 cm/½ inch of the potato on the skins. You can use the potato flesh to make mash.

3 Cut the skins into wedges. Put the remaining oil in a large bowl with the garlic, paprika and chilli flakes, if using, and mix until well combined. Season sparingly with salt and pepper.

4 Toss the potato wedges in the spicy oil, spread out on the baking sheet and bake in the oven for 20 minutes until the skins are brown and crisp.

5 Meanwhile make the dip. In a separate bowl mash the avocado with the lemon juice, then mash in the cheese and a little of the potato flesh until well combined and smooth.

6 Serve the spicy skins warm, piled up, with little pots of the dip.

Ham & Pineapple Muffin Pizzas

INGREDIENTS

makes 8

4 muffins

125 ml/4 fl oz ready-made tomato pizza sauce

2 sun-dried tomatoes in oil, chopped

55 g/2 oz Parma ham

2 rings canned pineapple, chopped

½ green pepper, deseeded and chopped

125 g/4½ oz mozzarella cheese, cubed

olive oil, for drizzling

salt and pepper

1 Preheat the grill to medium. Cut the muffins in half and toast the cut side lightly.

2 Spread the tomato sauce evenly over the muffins. Sprinkle the sun-dried tomatoes on top of the tomato sauce. Cut the Parma ham into thin strips and place on the muffins with the pineapple and pepper. Carefully arrange the mozzarella cubes on top.

3 Drizzle a little oil over each pizza and add salt and pepper to taste.

4 Place under the hot grill and cook until the cheese melts and bubbles. Serve immediately.

Oven-Fried Chicken Wings

INGREDIENTS

serves 4

12 chicken wings

1 egg

50 ml/2 fl oz milk

4 heaped tbsp plain flour

1 tsp paprika

225 g/8 oz breadcrumbs

55 g/2 oz butter

salt and pepper

1 Preheat the oven to 220°C/425°F/Gas Mark 7. Separate the chicken wings into 3 pieces each. Discard the bony tip. Beat the egg with the milk in a shallow dish. Combine the flour, paprika, and salt and pepper to taste in a separate shallow dish. Place the breadcrumbs in another shallow dish.

2 Dip the chicken pieces into the egg to coat well, then drain and roll in the seasoned flour. Remove, shaking off any excess, and roll the chicken in the breadcrumbs, gently pressing them onto the surface, then shaking off any excess breadcrumbs.

3 Melt the butter in the preheated oven in a shallow roasting tin large enough to hold all the chicken pieces in a single layer. Arrange the chicken, skin-side down, in the tin and bake in the oven for 10 minutes. Turn and bake for a further 10 minutes, or until the chicken is tender and the juices run clear when a skewer is inserted into the thickest part of the meat.

4 Remove the chicken from the tin and arrange on a large platter. Serve hot or at room temperature.

Nachos

INGREDIENTS

175 g/6 oz tortilla chips

400 g/14 oz canned refried beans, warmed

2 tbsp finely chopped bottled jalapeño chillies

200 g/7 oz canned or bottled pimentos or roasted peppers, drained and finely sliced

115 g/4 oz Gruyère cheese, grated

115 g/4 oz Cheddar cheese, grated

salt and pepper

serves 6

1 Preheat the oven to 200°C/400°F/Gas Mark 6.

2 Spread the tortilla chips out over the base of a large, shallow, ovenproof dish or roasting tin. Cover with the warmed refried beans. Scatter over the chillies and pimentos and season to taste with salt and pepper. Mix the cheeses together in a bowl and sprinkle on top.

3 Bake in the preheated oven for 5–8 minutes, or until the cheese is bubbling and melted. Serve immediately.

Fruity Dippers

INGREDIENTS

55 g/2 oz raspberries

1 tsp orange juice

2 tbsp natural or Greek-style yogurt

CHOOSE FROM FRUITS SUCH AS:

½ small banana, cut into chunks

½ dessert apple, peeled and cut into long slices

½ pear, peeled and cut into long slices

3–4 seedless grapes, halved

25 g/1 oz mango, cut into long thin slices

½ peach or nectarine, cut into slices

½ kiwi fruit, cut into sticks

serves 1–2

1 To make the dip, press the raspberries through a nylon sieve to remove the pips. Stir the raspberry purée and orange juice into the yogurt and spoon into a small dish. Arrange the fruits on a plate with the dip.

Apple Fritters

INGREDIENTS

serves 4

sunflower oil, for deep-frying

1 large egg

pinch of salt

175 ml/6 fl oz water

55 g/2 oz plain flour

2 tsp ground cinnamon

55 g/2 oz caster sugar

4 eating apples, peeled and cored

1 Pour the sunflower oil into a deep fryer or large, heavy-based saucepan and heat to 180–190°C/350–375°F, or until a cube of bread browns in 30 seconds.

2 Meanwhile, using an electric mixer, beat the egg and salt together until frothy, then quickly whisk in the water and flour. Do not overbeat the batter – it doesn't matter if it isn't completely smooth.

3 Mix the cinnamon and sugar together in a shallow dish and reserve.

4 Slice the apples into 5-mm/¼-inch thick rings. Spear with a fork, 1 slice at a time, and dip in the batter to coat. Add to the hot oil, in batches, and cook for 1 minute on each side, or until golden and puffed up. Remove with a slotted spoon and drain on kitchen paper. Keep warm while you cook the remaining batches. Transfer to a large serving plate, sprinkle with the cinnamon sugar and serve.

Chocolate Popcorn

INGREDIENTS

3 tbsp sunflower oil

70 g/2½ oz popcorn

25 g/1 oz butter

55 g/2 oz soft light brown sugar

2 tbsp golden syrup

1 tbsp milk

55 g/2 oz plain chocolate chips

serves 6–8

1 Preheat the oven to 150°C/300°F/Gas Mark 2. Heat the oil in a large, heavy-based saucepan. Add the popcorn, cover the pan, and cook, shaking the pan vigorously and frequently, for about 2 minutes, until the popping stops. Turn into a large bowl.

2 Put the butter, sugar, golden syrup and milk in a saucepan and heat gently until the butter has melted. Bring to the boil, without stirring, and boil for 2 minutes. Remove from the heat, add the chocolate chips, and stir until melted.

3 Pour the chocolate mixture over the popcorn and toss together until evenly coated. Spread the mixture onto a large baking tray.

4 Bake the popcorn in the oven for about 15 minutes, until crisp. Leave to cool before serving.

Oat Bars

INGREDIENTS

175 g/6 oz unsalted butter, plus extra for greasing

3 tbsp clear honey

150 g/5½ oz demerara sugar

100 g/3½ oz no-added-sugar smooth peanut butter

225 g/8 oz porridge oats

50 g/1¾ oz ready-to-eat dried apricots, chopped

2 tbsp sunflower seeds

2 tbsp sesame seeds

makes 16

1 Preheat the oven to 180°C/350°F/Gas Mark 4. Grease and line a 22-cm/8½-inch square baking tin.

2 Melt the butter, honey and sugar in a saucepan over a low heat. When the sugar has melted, add the peanut butter and stir until all the ingredients are well combined. Add all the remaining ingredients and mix well.

3 Press the mixture into the prepared tin and bake in the preheated oven for 20 minutes.

4 Remove from the oven and leave to cool in the tin, then cut into 16 squares.

6 Treats

Children love a dessert or snack as a treat and this chapter gives you plenty of ideas. Cutting cakes and biscuits into shapes such as stars or people will always attract youngsters, as does food that can be eaten easily with the fingers. Skewered fruit kebabs are ideal, and an excellent way of encouraging your children to eat fruit. Ice cream with whole strawberries or a gleaming strawberry sauce makes an extra-special treat for a birthday.

Apricot & Sunflower Seed Cookies

INGREDIENTS

100 g/3½ oz unsalted butter, softened

50 g/1¾ oz demerara sugar

1 tbsp maple syrup

1 tbsp honey, plus extra for brushing

1 large egg, beaten

100 g/3½ oz white plain flour, plus extra for dusting

150 g/5½ oz wholemeal plain flour

1 tbsp oat bran

50 g/1¾ oz ground almonds

1 tsp ground cinnamon

75 g/2¾ oz ready-to-eat dried apricots, chopped

25 g/1 oz sunflower seeds

makes 20

1 Beat the softened butter with the sugar in a large bowl until light and fluffy. Beat in the maple syrup and honey, then add the egg.

2 Add the flours and oat bran, then add the almonds and mix well. Add the cinnamon, apricots and seeds and, with floured hands, mix to a firm dough. Wrap in clingfilm and chill for 30 minutes.

3 Preheat the oven to 180°C/350°F/Gas Mark 4. Roll out the dough on a lightly floured work surface to 1 cm/½ inch thick. Using a 6 cm/2½ inch biscuit cutter, cut out 20 rounds, re-rolling the trimmings where possible, and place on a baking sheet. Brush with a little extra honey and bake in the preheated oven for 15 minutes until golden. Remove from the oven and leave to cool on a wire rack.

Orange & Banana Scones

INGREDIENTS

makes ❶❷

sunflower oil, for oiling

150 g/5½ oz white self-raising flour, plus extra for dusting, and for rolling, if needed

150 g/5½ oz light brown self-raising flour

1 tsp baking powder

½ tsp ground cinnamon

75 g/2¾ oz unsalted butter, diced and chilled

50 g/1¾ oz demerara sugar

150 ml/5 fl oz milk, plus extra for brushing

1 ripe banana, peeled and mashed

finely grated rind of 1 orange

150 g/5½ oz fresh raspberries, lightly mashed

1 Preheat the oven to 200°C/400°F/Gas Mark 6. Lightly oil a baking sheet.

2 Mix the flours, baking powder and cinnamon together in a large bowl, add the butter and rub in with your fingertips until the mixture resembles breadcrumbs. Stir in the sugar. Make a well in the middle and pour in the milk, add the banana and orange rind and mix to a soft dough. The dough will be quite wet.

3 Turn out the dough onto a lightly floured work surface and, adding a little more flour if needed, roll out to 2 cm/¾ inch thick. Using a 6 cm/2½ inch biscuit cutter, cut out 12 scones, re-rolling the trimmings where possible, and place them on the prepared baking sheet. Brush with milk and bake in the preheated oven for 10–12 minutes.

4 Remove from the oven and leave to cool slightly, then halve the scones and fill with the raspberries.

Gingerbread People

INGREDIENTS

makes 4 or more, depending on the size

175 g/6 oz plain flour

2 tsp ground ginger

½ tsp bicarbonate of soda

55 g/2 oz butter or margarine

85 g/3 oz soft brown sugar

2 tbsp golden syrup

1 egg, beaten

Smarties and jelly orange and lemon cake decorations, to decorate

1 Preheat the oven to 190°C/375°F/Gas Mark 5. Sift the flour, ginger and bicarbonate of soda into a large mixing bowl. Add the butter and rub into the flour with your fingertips until it resembles fine breadcrumbs. Mix in the sugar.

2 Warm the syrup in a small saucepan until runny, then add to the flour mixture with the beaten egg. Mix to form a soft dough, then knead lightly until smooth. If the dough is too sticky, add a little extra flour.

3 Roll out the dough on a lightly floured work surface then, using a cutter, make the gingerbread people. Place on a lightly greased baking sheet and cook for 10 minutes, or until just crisp and golden. Allow to cool.

4 Use the Smarties to make eyes and buttons, and attach the jelly orange and lemon cake decorations to make a mouth.

Apple & Blueberry with Oaty Cobbler Topping

INGREDIENTS

200 g/7 oz mixed dessert apple and blueberries

pinch of ground cinnamon

1 tsp caster sugar

COBBLER TOPPING

40 g/1½ oz plain flour

½ tsp baking powder

2 tsp caster sugar

25 g/1 oz unsalted butter

50 ml/2 fl oz soured cream

1 tbsp rolled oats

serves 2

1 Preheat the oven to 200°C/400°F/Gas Mark 6. Put the fruit, cinnamon and sugar into a small saucepan with 1 tablespoon water. Heat gently and cook for a few minutes until the fruit begins to soften. Remove from the heat.

2 Divide the fruit between two individual ovenproof dishes. Put the flour, baking powder, sugar and butter into a small bowl and rub in until the mixture resembles fresh breadcrumbs. Mix in the soured cream. Put the rolled oats on a saucer, then drop teaspoonfuls of the mixture on top and roll in the oats. Flatten the pieces slightly and arrange on top of the fruit. Put the dishes on a baking sheet and bake for about 20 minutes until golden brown.

Fragrant Rice Pudding

INGREDIENTS

serves 2–3

5 g/2 oz short-grain pudding rice

300 ml/10 fl oz full-fat milk

seeds from 1 cardamom pod, crushed

½ tsp vanilla extract

2 tsp sugar (optional)

milk or orange juice, for thinning (optional)

1 large orange, peel and pith removed and cut into segments

1 tsp clear honey

few drops of orange flower water

1 Put the rice, milk, crushed cardamom seeds, vanilla extract and sugar, if using, into a small saucepan. Bring to the boil and simmer very gently for about 20 minutes, stirring frequently. When the rice grains are very soft, remove from the heat and leave to cool. Thin with a little milk or orange juice if necessary.

2 Put the orange segments into a dish and drizzle over the honey and orange flower water. Toss gently together and serve with the rice pudding.

Ice Cream with Strawberry Sauce & Star Biscuits

INGREDIENTS

600 ml/1 pint double cream

1 vanilla pod, split

4 egg yolks

55 g/2 oz caster sugar

175 g/6 oz strawberries

1 tbsp icing sugar

STAR BISCUITS

55 g/2 oz icing sugar, sifted

85 g/3 oz unsalted butter, softened

1 egg yolk

140 g/5 oz plain flour, plus extra for dusting

serves 6–8

1 Put the cream into a saucepan. Scrape the seeds from the vanilla pod and add them to the saucepan, together with the pod. Bring to the boil, remove from the heat and leave for about 20 minutes.

2 Mix together the egg yolks and caster sugar. Pour on the cream. Return the mixture to the cleaned saucepan and cook very gently until the mixture starts to thicken, stirring constantly. Pass through a sieve into a bowl. Cover and leave until cold.

3 Churn the mixture in an ice cream maker, or pour into a bowl and freeze. When it is half frozen, remove and whisk. Return to the freezer. Repeat 4 or 5 times.

4 To make the sauce, put the strawberries and icing sugar into a bowl and purée using a hand blender.

5 To make the star biscuits, preheat the oven to 180°C/350°F/Gas Mark 4. Put all the ingredients into a bowl and mix until a smooth dough is formed. Roll out on a floured surface and cut out small star shapes. Place on a non-stick baking sheet and bake for 5–10 minutes until golden brown. Serve the ice cream with the sauce and the star biscuits.

Baby Baked Apples with Fudge Yogurt

INGREDIENTS

200 ml/7 fl oz whipping cream

200 ml/7 fl oz natural Greek-style yogurt

4 tbsp soft dark brown sugar

4 small dessert apples

8 ready-to-eat dried apricots, chopped

2 tsp butter

serves 4

1 To make the fudge yogurt, whisk the whipping cream until thick. Fold in the yogurt and put into a bowl. Sprinkle over the brown sugar then cover and chill in the refrigerator for 1 hour. During chilling the sugar will liquefy and form a thin layer of 'sauce'.

2 Preheat the oven to 200°C/400°F/Gas Mark 6.

3 Wash the apples and remove the cores. Using a sharp knife, make an incision round each apple about halfway up, so the apple can expand during baking. Put the apples in a small ovenproof dish and fill the centres with the apricots. Put a knob of butter on top of each one and bake in the oven for about 15 minutes, or until soft.

4 Swirl the liquefied sugar through the yogurt and serve with the warm apples.

Sugar-Frosted Fruit Pie

INGREDIENTS

serves 6

350 g/12 oz self-raising flour

175 g/6 oz butter

water, for mixing and brushing

1 tbsp cornflour

100 g/3½ oz caster sugar

1 tsp ground cinnamon

finely grated rind of 1 small orange

finely grated rind of 1 small lemon

8 Granny Smith apples, peeled, cored and sliced

2 tsp lemon juice

cream, ice cream or custard, to serve

TOPPING

1 egg white, beaten until frothy

1 tbsp caster sugar

1 Preheat the oven to 200°C/400°F/Gas Mark 6. Place a baking sheet in the oven.

2 Put the flour into a bowl and rub in the butter until the mixture resembles fine breadcrumbs. Add enough water to mix to a soft but not sticky dough. Roll out just under half the dough on a floured surface and use to line the base of a 22-cm/9-inch pie plate.

3 Mix together the cornflour, sugar, cinnamon and orange and lemon rinds and toss together with the apples and lemon juice. Pile the mixture into the pastry-lined dish. Dampen the edge of the pastry with water. Roll out the remaining pastry and use to cover the pie. Roll out any trimmings and cut out leaf shapes. Brush these with water and attach them to the pie. Brush the top of the pie with beaten egg white and sprinkle with sugar. Place the pie on the hot baking tray in the oven and cook for about 30–40 minutes until golden brown. Serve with cream, ice cream or custard.

Chocolate Mousse

INGREDIENTS

serves 6

100 g/3½ oz plain chocolate (minimum 70% cocoa solids), chopped

1 tbsp butter

2 large eggs, separated

1 tbsp maple syrup

2 tbsp Greek-style yogurt

100 g/3½ oz blueberries

1 tbsp water

25 g/1 oz white chocolate, grated

1 Put the chocolate and butter in a heatproof bowl, set the bowl over a saucepan of barely simmering water and heat until melted. Leave to cool slightly, then stir in the egg yolks, maple syrup and yogurt.

2 Whisk the egg whites in a large, grease-free bowl until stiff, then fold into the chocolate mixture. Divide between 6 small ramekins and chill for 4 hours.

3 Meanwhile, put the blueberries in a small saucepan with the water and cook until the berries begin to pop and turn glossy. Leave to cool, then chill.

4 To serve, top each mousse with a few blueberries and a little white chocolate.

Strawberry Yogurt Lollies

INGREDIENTS

350 g/12 oz fresh strawberries, hulled and sliced

300 g/10½ oz thick natural yogurt

3 tbsp honey

few drops of vanilla extract

makes 10

1 Put the strawberries, yogurt, honey and vanilla essence in a blender and process until puréed.

2 Pour the mixture into ice lolly moulds and freeze until solid. (Fun-shaped moulds are popular.)

Mini Strawberry Cheesecakes

INGREDIENTS

75 g/2¾ oz unsalted butter

75 g/2¾ oz rolled oats

25 g/1 oz chopped hazelnuts

225 g/8 oz ricotta cheese

50 g/1¾ oz demerara sugar

finely grated rind of 1 lemon, and juice of ½ lemon

1 egg, plus 1 egg yolk

150 g/5½ oz cottage cheese

1 kiwi fruit

6 large strawberries

makes 6

1 Line 6 holes of a muffin tin with muffin paper cases.

2 Melt the butter in a small saucepan over a low heat, then leave to cool. Put the oats in a food processor and pulse briefly to break them up, then tip into a bowl, add the nuts and melted butter and mix well. Divide the mixture between the paper cases and press down well. Chill for 30 minutes.

3 Preheat the oven to 150°C/300°F/Gas Mark 2. Beat the ricotta cheese with the sugar, and lemon rind and juice, in a bowl. Add the egg, egg yolk and cottage cheese and mix well. Spoon into the muffin cases and bake in the preheated oven for 30 minutes. Turn off the oven, but leave the cheesecakes in the oven until completely cold.

4 Peel the kiwi fruit and slice the flesh, and halve the strawberries. Remove the paper cases, top each cheesecake with the fruit and serve.

Ice Cream Strawberry Sundae

INGREDIENTS

serves 4

8 scoops of good-quality vanilla ice cream

25 g/1 oz chopped mixed nuts, lightly toasted in a dry frying pan

marshmallows and grated chocolate, to serve

STRAWBERRY SAUCE

250 g/9 oz strawberries, hulled and halved

2 tbsp freshly squeezed orange juice

2 tbsp caster sugar

1 To make the sauce, put the strawberries in a blender with the orange juice and process until smooth. Transfer the mixture to a saucepan and add the sugar. Cook over a medium heat for 10–12 minutes, or until thickened. Leave to cool.

2 To serve, place a spoonful of the strawberry sauce in the bottom of a tall glass. Add two scoops of ice cream and another spoonful of fruit sauce. Sprinkle with the nuts and chocolate. Arrange the marshmallows on top. Repeat to make four sundaes.

Fruit Skewers

INGREDIENTS

serves 4

selection of fruit, such as apricots, peaches, figs, strawberries, mangoes, pineapple, bananas, dates and pawpaw, prepared and cut into chunks

maple syrup, to taste

50 g/1¾ oz plain chocolate (minimum 70% cocoa solids), broken into chunks

1 Soak 4 bamboo skewers in water for at least 20 minutes.

2 Preheat the grill to high and line the grill pan with foil. Thread pieces of fruit onto each skewer. Brush the fruit with a little maple syrup.

3 Put the chocolate in a heatproof bowl, set the bowl over a saucepan of barely simmering water and heat until it is melted.

4 Meanwhile, cook the skewers under the preheated grill for 3 minutes, or until caramelized. Serve drizzled with a little of the melted chocolate, removing the fruit from the skewer if serving to younger children.

Index